Scary Stories of Mammoth Cave

Scary Stories of Mammoth Cave

by

Colleen O'Connor Olson
with the assistance of Charles Hanion

Illustrations by Roger W. Brucker

CAVE BOOKS
Dayton, Ohio

Published by CAVE BOOKS
4700 Amberwood Drive
Dayton, OH 45424, USA
www.cavebooks.com

CAVE BOOKS is the publications affiliate of the Cave
Research Foundation.

Editor: Richard Watson
Publisher: Roger McClure
Layout and Typesetting: Paul Steward
Cover Graphic Design: Gary Berdeaux
Cover Photograph: Robert Cetera
Illustrations: Roger Brucker

Library of Congress Cataloging-in-Publication Data

Olson, Colleen O'Connor, 1966-
    Scary stories from Mammoth Cave / by Colleen O'Connor
Olson ; with the assistance of Charles Hanion ; illustrations
by Roger Brucker.
    p. cm.
    Includes bibliographical references.
    Contents: Lost – An experiment in the dark – Displays of
the dead – Ghosts – Floyd – Hellish names – Just plain
unusual.
    ISBN 0-939748-54-1 (pbk. : alk. Paper)
    1. Mammoth Cave (Ky.)–History–Anecdotes. 2.
Mammoth Cave (KY.)–Anecdotes. 3. Ghosts–Kentucky–
Mammoth Cave–Anecdotes. 4. Curiosities and wonders–
Kentucky–Mammoth Cave–Anecdotes. 5. Mammoth Cave
(Ky.)–Fiction. 6. Ghost stories, American–Kentucky–
Mammoth Cave. I. Hanion, Charles, 1954- II. Title.

F457.M2 O45 2002976.9'754–dc21

                                          2002073806

To my husband Rick Olson, who was helpful in so many ways. –Colleen O'Connor Olson

To Penny for all the years, and to my Mammoth Cave family. –Charles Hanion

ACKNOWLEDGMENTS

The following people helped to make this book possible: Robert Cetera for taking the cover photograph, Zona Cetera, Gary Berdoux, and Keven Neff for assisting with the photography; Robert Cetera, Zona Cetera, Candice Leek, Lewis Cutliff, George Deike, Sarah Flowers, Jaime Gray, Joy Medley Lyons, Michael Nardacci, Arthur Palmer, Neila Spradlin, William White, Kerry Wood, and George Wood, for telling me about their personal experiences in the Mammoth Cave system; Paul G. Anderson, Don Coons, Eugene Conner, Stanley Sides, Chuck DeCroix, Joseph Lawrence, Michelle Karle, Arthur Palmer, Margaret Palmer, Gordon Smith, Samantha Teodorski, and Richard Watson for providing information; Sue Hagan, Penny Gibson Hanion, Joy Medley Lyons, Caroline McCombs, Davis McCombs, Rick Olson, Michael Sutton, and Heather Woodruff for reviewing the manuscript.

CONTENTS

PREFACE

Among the many intriguing mysteries of Mammoth Cave are sightings of ghostly figures that appear now and again along major tour routes. Perhaps they watch us through a portal in time, long separated from the physical world in which the living reside. They belong to the shadows and darkness of the cave world, and to the human mind, which catches glimpses of these denizens of the netherworld. Perhaps they are simply projections of our own fears and imaginations.

The stories in this book provide glimpses into this shadowy world of Mammoth Cave. Illumination is provided only by the flame of our desire to know what the cave itself knows.

LOST

Ah, so this is your first trip into the cave. As you enter Mammoth Cave's long, dark, mysterious passages, a number of nervous thoughts go through your head. "Will I fit through the tight places?" You notice several people bigger than you on the tour and figure that if they will fit, so will you. "What if I fall down the Bottomless Pit!?" There are handrails, what a relief. "A rock might fall on my head!" The ranger assures you that no rocks have fallen on anybody in modern times (however long that is). But you are feeling more at ease. Then you notice dozens of side passages. The ranger says the cave is more than 350 miles long! That is when your worst fear comes to mind. "What if I get LOST!?"

The odds of accidentally wandering down the wrong passage on a modern cave tour are low, but the thought of doing so has worried Mammoth Cave visitors since the early nineteenth century. In his *A Guide Manual to the Mammoth Cave of Kentucky*, published in 1860, Charles Wright warns of unpleasant consequences for those who wander astray.

A person lost in the Mammoth Cave, without any hope of escape, would undoubtedly die in a very short time. That this is the case, the history of those who have been lost in it would seem to prove.

Thus, on one occasion a gentleman wandered from his party, when by some accident his lamp was extinguished. In endeavoring to make his escape, he became alarmed, and finally insane, and crawling behind a large rock, remained in that position for forty-eight hours; and although guides repeatedly passed the rock behind which he was secreted, in search of him, he did not make the slightest noise, and when finally discovered, endeavored to make his escape from them, but was too much exhausted to run.

In another instance a lady allowed her party to get so far in advance that their voices could no longer be heard, and in attempt to overtake them, fell and extinguished her lamp, she became so terrified at her situation that she swooned, and when discovered a few minutes afterward, and restored, was found to be in a state of insanity, from which she did not recover for a number of years.[1]

In 1880, Horace C. Hovey mentioned a close brush with disaster caused by someone leaving the group.

We witnessed, one day, a narrow escape on the part of an excitable gentleman, who trusted to his own guidance. His companions were following their guide up the chimney-like corkscrew, and he caught at

2

the bright idea of getting ahead of them by the longer route. He started off alone and on the full run. We followed him more out of curiosity than apprehension. His lamp went out; but in his eagerness he did not stop to relight it, relying on the scattered rays of ours behind him. Suddenly Tom darted forward and grasped the stranger in his strong arms. We abruptly halted. There, within a single step, yawned the Sidesaddle Pit, on whose black rocks, a hundred feet below, the man would have fallen, had it not been for Tom's presence of mind.[2]

Perhaps telling of the misfortunes of those that ventured forward or lagged behind was the nineteenth century guides' way of discouraging visitors from leaving the safety of the group.

H.P. Lovecraft, a well-known author of the macabre in the early twentieth century, may have had a guide who used this preventive measure on a visit to Mammoth Cave. In his short story, "The Beast in the Cave," the main character sees the worst possible result of leaving the group.

I was lost, completely, hopelessly lost in the vast and labyrinthine recesses of the Mammoth Cave. . . .

My disaster was the result of no fault save my own, since unbeknown to the guide I had separated myself from the regular party of sightseers; and, wandering for over an hour in forbidden avenues of the cave, had found myself unable to trace the devious windings which I had pursued since forsaking my companions.

He soon realizes he is not alone.

> I was now convinced I had by my cries
> aroused and attracted some wild beast.
> .... I wondered what species of animal was to
> confront me; it must, I thought, be some
> unfortunate beast who had paid for its curi-
> osity to investigate one of the entrances of
> the fearful grotto with a lifelong confine-
> ment in its interminable recesses.

He has the good fortune to mortally wound the beast that is stalking him. Seconds later he is found by his guide. The two go forth to examine the animal:

> ... of all the unnatural monsters either of us
> had in our lifetimes beheld, this was in sur-
> passing degree the strangest. It appeared to
> be an anthropoid ape of large proportions,
> escaped, perhaps, from some itinerant me-
> nagerie. Its hair was snow-white, a thing due
> no doubt to the bleaching action of a long
> existence in the cave, but it was also sur-
> prisingly thin, being indeed largely absent
> save on the head, where it was of such
> length and abundance that it fell over the
> shoulders in considerable profusion. ... No
> tail seemed to be present.
> As we gazed upon the uncanny sight
> presented to our vision, the thick lips
> opened, and several *sounds* issued from
> them, after which the *thing* relaxed in death.
> Then fear left, and wonder, awe, com-
> passion, and reverence succeeded in its
> place, for the *sounds* uttered by the stricken
> figure that lay stretched out on the lime-
> stone had told us the awesome truth. The

creature I had killed, the strange beast of the unfathomed cave was, or had at one time been, a MAN!!![3]

Mammoth Cave's multitude of passages, crawlways, chambers, and avenues give even those who are familiar with the cave opportunity to get lost. In 1900, Curtis G. Lloyd, a frequent Mammoth Cave visitor, was on a trip destined for Echo River in the lowest level of the cave. Lloyd informed his guide he was going to separate from the group (first mistake), take a shortcut through a crazy jumble of tumbledown boulders known as the Corkscrew (second mistake), and meet the party at the river. When the main party reached Echo River, Lloyd was nowhere to be seen. The guide, knowing Lloyd knew his way around, assumed he must have already been to the river and returned to the surface. But when they got back above ground, there was no Lloyd. A search party went into the Corkscrew to find him. Twelve hours later they found a jittery Lloyd, sitting smoking cigars a mere fifty feet from where the tour party had passed on their way back from Echo River. Lloyd's feelings about the incident are expressed on the wall:[4]

Lost Chamber
It is Hell to be Lost
3 Hours Here
C,,G,,L,,[5]

Perhaps Lloyd spent the first nine hours doing a little exploring before coming to the conclusion that he was lost.

According to Robert Bird in his 1838 book *Peter Pilgrim*, staying with your guide is no guarantee you will not get lost. Two visitors and their guide walked into Wright's Rotunda, a room so great in size the lights from their lanterns could scarcely reveal all within (modern visitors also see Wright's Rotunda by the flicker of a lantern on the Violet City Lantern Tour). They went to the Black Chambers, a passage leading out of Wright's Rotunda. Finding one's way into the Black Chambers is an easy task. The way out, however, is not so clear. Because of the jumble of rocks around the chimney-like exit passage, the poor guide became confused as to where it was. The group feared they were not only lost, but also trapped by a rock fall.

> Here was a situation: and soon there was a scene. The young gentlemen became frantic; and declaring they would sooner die on the spot than endure their horrible imprisonment longer, condemned to agonize out existence by inches, they drew their pistols—with which, like true American travelers, they were both well provided—resolving at once to end the catastrophe. The only difficulty was a question that occurred, whether each should do execution upon himself by blowing his own brains out, or whether, devoted to friendship even in death, each should do that office for the other. Fortunately, before the difficulty was settled, the guide stumbled upon one of the Chimneys, and blood and gunpowder were both saved.[6]

As you stroll down Main Cave, the large passage on the Violet City Lantern Tour, you may glance to your right and notice a low passage leading someplace. The guide says it is called Harvey's Avenue. What did Harvey do to earn the honor of having a passage named after him? Was he a great cave explorer? A past owner of Mammoth Cave? No, he just got lost.

In the late 1830s, Charles Harvey, Jr., the nephew of

Charles Harvey, Jr. has a bad day
underground.

Mammoth Cave's owner Franklin Gorin, ventured down Main Cave with his father Charles Harvey, Sr. Father and son stopped for a drink of water at a spring where Charles, Jr. took off his hat and left it. Later in the journey he realized he had forgotten his hat and went back to retrieve it. While catching up with his father, Charles took a wrong turn down the passage that is today affectionately named after him. After searching in vain, Charles, Sr. went for help. Thirty-nine hours later a very frightened Charles Harvey, Jr. was found.[7]

A possibly embellished version of this true story is that the rescuers heard the sound of two rocks knocking together, echoing through the cave. They followed the noise until they found Charles, Jr. sitting on the ground banging on rocks. "You certainly are a smart man to make noise so we could find you," proclaimed his rescuers. "I was not beating on rocks so you would hear me," replied Charles, Jr. "The infernal silence of the cave would have driven me insane without some noise!"

Getting lost was not always accidental. A fictional tale of a young woman's unrequited love tells of how she lost the man who did not return her affection. He had proclaimed his love for another. So while they were in a Mammoth Cave passage known as Purgatory, she abandoned him.

> I felt a savage delight in the fright, the terror, the despair into which I had plunged him. I knew there would be hours of searching before he could be found, and I thought of the tortures he was enduring with positive delight. But I never dreamed of his death. No! I can truly say, that the idea of that never crossed my mind. I had quitted him in one of the thoroughfares of the Cave, the most likely place to be searched. When I left him there alone, I had no

thought but of the dreaded hours of loneli-
ness, which would seem like ages to him
that must elapse before he was discovered
by his friends. No one, to my knowledge,
had ever been entirely lost in the Cave; and
I never contemplated the possibility that he
would head the list of those who have perished in that awful darkness and silence.

The guilt over her love's death drove her to seek the
same fate for herself.

I am going to reenter that dark Cave, the
threshold of which I have not crossed for
fifteen years, and there I will patiently await
the coming of that death, which I hope to
me will be a blessed release. The gloom and
horror to which, years ago, I doomed my
victim, shall be around me when I die: for I
think that perhaps from amid the silent
rocks which witnessed my crime, my last
prayer for forgiveness will find acceptance.

Modern visitors to Mammoth Cave have claimed to
hear the voice of the ghost of the lost man calling for the
broken hearted young woman to come to his rescue.
This seems unlikely given that this story, "A Tragedy of
the Mammoth Cave," was made up for *The Knickerbocker* magazine in 1858.[8]

As you leave the dark confines of the cave and walk
up into the sunny surface world, you laugh at yourself
for worrying so much about getting lost. Yet, as you mull
over stories of unfortunate souls going insane or com-
pleting life underground, you can't help but wonder,
"Weren't there more people in the tour group on the
way in?"

AN EXPERIMENT IN THE DARK

In 1839, Mammoth Cave was purchased by Dr. John Croghan, a medical doctor living in Louisville, Kentucky. Croghan was a nephew of Revolutionary War hero General George Rogers Clark and of explorer William Clark, of Lewis and Clark fame. Dr. Croghan was an adventurous man who possessed the restless traits of his famous uncles. He was also prone to dabbling in various enterprises, including interests as diverse as salt mining and farming.

Croghan had two great plans for Mammoth Cave. First, he wished to make the cave more attractive to visitors by improving trails and access to the cave, including the stagecoach route leading to the surface hotel. He then proposed to increase accommodations by constructing a health resort within the cave's interior, reachable by underground carriage. This idea was accompanied by grandiose ideas for band performances, refreshments, and even a Fourth of July fireworks celebration inside the cave.[9]

The dryness of the cave interior, the remarkable preservation of the wooden timbers from the saltpeter mining operations, and the relatively stable temperature and humidity all played a role in the development of the second, and more bizarre phase of his plan.

After having read reports published in the *Medical Repository* of 1815 that attest to the good health of the slaves who worked the saltpeter mines in the cave during the War of 1812, Croghan theorized that the cave must surely possess curative properties.[10]

He also knew that during the 1820s, Nathan Gaither, M.D., from Columbia, Kentucky, had proposed that the Commonwealth of Kentucky purchase Mammoth Cave to establish a hospital in one of its corridors. Another medical doctor, Robert Montgomery Bird, former professor at Pennsylvania Medical College, visited Mammoth Cave in 1833 and 1836. He published an article in the magazine *American Monthly* of 1837 to advertise the wonders of Mammoth Cave and to extol the medical benefits of the cave air. Bird made a comment later referred to by Dr. Croghan: "I recommend all broken hearted lovers and dyspeptic dandies to carry their complaints to the Mammoth Cave, where they will undoubtedly find themselves translated into very buxom and happy persons before they are aware of it."[11]

In his *The Principal Diseases of the Interior Valley of North America* of 1850, Daniel Drake makes a reference to the health of the slaves who worked in Mammoth Cave as saltpeter miners:

> It was observed that the health of the operatives was excellent and that many ailing or weakly persons became sound in health, and experienced increase of flesh. The oxen . . . became fat. With these facts before their eyes, the people near the cave have long believed that it might be made an advantageous abode for invalids, especially those affected with pulmonary

diseases, as they would escape all vicissitudes of temperature.[12]

Franklin Gorin, who sold the cave to Croghan in 1839, wrote about the health of the nitrate miners, stating that "some worked in the cave without coming out for an entire year . . . coming out healthy, and having a beautiful gloss with shining faces and skins."[13]

The following year, however, Dr. Robert Davidson was less enthusiastic about the living conditions inside the cave. Referring to Wandering Willie, the travelling minstrel from Cincinnati, Davidson wrote: "As for passing the night there, most persons would be deterred by fear of dampness; and still fewer would be affected by the sole stimulus of an excited curiosity. Burning to feel the sublimity which he imagined the solitude and total darkness would create, the young man spent the night in the cave by a pool, but was kept awake by the bats flying over his face."[14]

In 1841, Dr. William McDowell, a Louisville physician with a particular interest in the treatment of phthisis or tuberculosis, referred to then as consumption, had sought to utilize the cave environment for one of his woman patients. He published a book in 1843 entitled *A Demonstration of the Curability of Pulmonary Consumption in All Its Stages*, which was controversial, since he claimed that consumption was curable and suggested that salt and iron would be beneficial in its cure. No doubt other doctors of the day hoped they would find the cure, and were unhappy that McDowell was ahead of the game.

Croghan had made the acquaintance of Dr. McDowell, who helped him in his establishment of the underground hospital. Thus the stage was set for the second phase of Dr. Croghan's plan—the placement of invalids in the cave for treatment of "pulmonary afflictions." But Croghan did not begin development until the spring of 1842, due to illnesses within his family.

McDowell had promised Croghan that as many as a hundred invalids would visit the cave for treatment of various diseases. But by January, 1843, the actual number to arrive at the cave was around fifteen. These included several of the patients' wives, an attendant, and a small child (not considered to be a patient).[15]

A series of wooden huts, some roofed with canvas for privacy, were built in the cave for the patients to live in. Two stone buildings, referred to as "consumptive cabins" on postcards published a century ago, remain in the cave today. The following excerpt from Horace Hovey's *Guide Book to the Mammoth Cave of Kentucky* of 1882, details the buildings:

> The roofless remains of two stone buildings are next visited, as having a melancholy interest on account of their history. These and ten frame ones, now torn down were built for the use of consumptive patients, who here took up their abode. The second stone house was a dining room, all the rest were lodging rooms, and were well-furnished. They stood in a line, about 30 feet apart, from the acute angle onward. The cottages were not all at this spot.[16]

Dr. William R. Mitchill, from Glasgow, Kentucky was the first patient to live in the cave, only a few hundred yards from the natural entrance, in Audubon Avenue. He stayed in his wooden structure from May 23 to June 25, 1842. He had diagnosed his ailment as tuberculosis. After only one month he pronounced himself "cured" and left the cave. He was in the advanced stages of the disease. Although Mitchill apparently benefited from being in the cave, William Jones notes in his 1844 book, *Wonderful Curiosity: A Correct Narrative of Celebrated*

Mammoth Cave's underground tuberculosis
hospital.

Mammoth Cave of Kentucky, the following about him:

> After spending some weeks in his sub-
> terranean abode, he removed to Glasgow
> and in a short while sunk under his disease.
> Many persons believed that inhaling the
> cave air would effectually cure diseases of
> the lungs, which belief is erroneous. Yet it is
> undoubtedly beneficial to persons thus af-
> flicted, and indeed to any person of a weak
> and delicate constitution; and would dis-
> eased persons remain entirely within the
> cave, their health would be improved and
> their life prolonged.[17]

Mitchell died in the winter of 1842, a few months after leaving the cave for Glasgow. But not before plans were made for the arrival of other consumptive patients to Mammoth Cave. Croghan had constructed several small cottages in Audubon Avenue by this time. The second patient to arrive wished to reside further in the cave, away from the draughts of the entrance. This was John Wesley Harper from South Carolina, who arrived on September 15, 1842. He lived in solitude with his disease in a structure nearly 2,000 feet from the cave mouth, at Wandering Willie Spring in the Main Cave avenue known as Broadway. He died in the cave on January 18, 1843.

One month after Harper began living in his solitude, Oliver Hazard Perry Anderson entered the cave as the first patient to reside in the series of huts built near the present day stone cottage remains near the Star Chamber. He said his cabin was 12 by 18 feet with walls and floor of wood, and a roof made from canvas.

Anderson decided to leave the cave because of smoke from the grease lamps and cooking fires, but before doing so he described the gloomy conditions experienced by the patients:

Our hours are those of the upper world
indicated by our watches; a taper burns at
night, and two stearine lights in the day; we
walk with lamps furnished with lard oil and
I seldom hear daylight mentioned and for
myself seldom think of it; the endless interest of this novel place keeps us rambling
and when fatigued, books, papers or letters
or social visits fill up the time.

Croghan constructed a cabin in a lower passage of
the cave, known as Pensico Avenue, because he thought
the air there was even more invigorating than in the
upper levels. Anderson asked to live in that passage. He
soon moved back to Star Chamber, however. He com-
plained of the damper and colder conditions in the
lower level passage that increased his personal misery.
After the death of two of his fellow patients, he decided
to leave the subterranean hospital, which was fast
becoming a morgue.

The day after his departure, Anderson wrote a letter
to Henry Wingate, a Frankfort gentleman, concerning
the sale of Anderson's property and house:

I left the cave yesterday under the im-
pression that I would be better out than in
as my lungs were constantly irritated with
smoke and my nose offended by a disagree-
able effluvia, the necessary consequence of
its being so tenanted without ventilation.

When I came out, I cannot tell you
how delightful the upper world was to all
my senses. The air was sweet, pure, and
agreeable and the light to my surprise did
not hurt my eyes.

I would not have left the cave had I
calculated on better weather, but I shall try
to be as careful of consequences as I can

be. I am sure I am better out than in if I
take no heavy cold to settle on my lungs
and I feel some considerable hope from
the pleasant effect thus far that I will. I
don't look as well as when I entered the
cave. Others will leave the cave soon, I
think. Two recently died. I am the 5th person who was left.[18]

O. H. P. Anderson died in May, 1845, and was buried in the Frankfort, Kentucky Cemetery, not far from
the monument to Daniel Boone.

The suffering of the remaining tuberculosis patients
was great. Their condition deteriorated rather than
improved, as indicated by testimonials from writers of
the era:

Those patients who remained in the cave
three or four months, presented a fright-
ening appearance. The face was entirely
bloodless, eyes sunken, and the pupils di-
lated to such a degree that the iris ceased
to be visible, so that, no matter what the
original color of the eye might have been,
it soon appeared black.[19]

They lost every particle of flesh; crept
gloomily about, coughing so hollowly as to
suggest the sound of the first earth falling
upon a coffin-lid; and added to the natural
dreariness of the vault a hundred-fold.
Everybody saw and knew that they were
tottering on the brink of the grave; and yet,
such was their hope . . . that they could not
be persuaded to quit that purgatory. They
even imagined they were improving, and
insisted that they were stronger, when they

could not drag their leaden limbs after them.[20]

> I can conceive of one man being bene-
> fited by a residence in the cave, but the
> idea of a company of lank cadaverous in-
> valids wandering about in the awful gloom
> and silence, broken only by their hollow
> coughs—double hollow and sepulchral
> there—is terrible.[21]

Meanwhile, tours continued through the cave, past the wood and stone buildings of the consumptive patients. One can easily imagine the surprise awaiting visitors to the cave during 1842 and 1843. In the bleak distance, ghostly apparitions would seem to float between the buildings. As one approached these ghosts, they would become more solid and would reveal themselves to be alive, although the ghastly expressions of suffering on their faces showed that the essence of life was draining slowly from their bodies.

In another account, a death scene is tragically described:

> Another patient, who went in and re-
> mained some weeks, was attended by
> friends and a servant—but, his end ap-
> proaching, the death-scene in that dark and
> silent abyss became so appalling, that they
> fled in terror—friends and servant—and
> left the dying man alone. Nothing could
> induce them to return, and, when others
> went in, the poor man was found dead
> with an expression of indescribable horror
> upon his features.[22]

Visitors to Mammoth Cave today can still see the silent testimonials of An Experiment in the Dark. Two stone consumptive cabins remain, one of which stands beside a slab of stone known as Corpse Rock. The bodies of the patients who had succumbed to their disease were laid out on it until they were removed for burial.

One can also visit the Old Guide's Cemetery, a short walk from the visitor center. Besides seeing the final resting place of Stephen Bishop, the most famous cave guide from the 1800s, you can also visit the graves of the three tuberculosis patients known to have died in the cave during Croghan's experiment.

Although the hospital was deemed to be a good idea by many doctors of the day, the personal accounts of the patients and observers, and the deaths of patients within the cave, led to criticism of the experiment. In 1849, Croghan himself died of tuberculosis.

DISPLAYS OF THE DEAD

Human preoccupation with death and the after-life is as old as the first person who was buried in the earth. Mammoth Cave has its own peculiar legacy pertaining to the fascination with death. According to archeological studies, prehistoric Indians first entered the great natural entrance of Mammoth Cave nearly 4,000 years ago. Their use of the cave ended nearly 2,000 years ago.

Evidence left scattered along the dry, boulder-strewn cave passages include the remains of cane torches and slippers hand-woven from plant fibers from the forest. Telltale peck marks on the cave walls indicate where cave minerals were removed by prehistoric mining. Crusts of gypsum and other natural salts still line walls and ceilings that are thick with soot from burning torches.

Soon after settlers rediscovered the natural entrance of Mammoth Cave during the late 1790s, evidence of these prehistoric explorers was noticed. In the early 1800s, three prehistoric bodies, referred to as mummies, were found by nitrate miners in Short Cave, approximately seven miles from Mammoth Cave.

The first mummy found in Short Cave was the body of an infant buried very close to the entrance inside the cave. It was discovered around 1811. During excavation, the body was accidentally destroyed and thrown out with the rock debris from the cave. A letter from that era reveals the following:

> The atmosphere of these caves prevents all putrefaction. Dead bodies have been found which when first seen, were apparently as perfect as at the period when deposited there. A child was lately dug up in a cave wrapped up in cloth described as resembling canvas, enveloped in deer skin. The corpse appeared as if newly dead but upon exposure to the open atmosphere in a few hours crumbled into dust.[23]

The body of an adult male was discovered shortly thereafter and became a prominent exhibit at Scudder's Museum in New York City. It became known as the Scudder Mummy. It was seen by Constantine Samuel Rafinesque, a brilliant and eccentric naturalist of the day. While visiting the museum in 1818, he drew an illustration of the mummy. This drawing was published in the *Medical Repository* by Dr. Samuel L. Mitchell.[24] Mitchell subsequently wrote the following letter to a friend in 1815, in which he describes the mummy:

> I offer you some observations on a curious piece of American antiquity now in New York. It is a human body found in one of the limestone caverns of Kentucky. The body is in a squatting posture, with the right arm reclining forward, and its hand encircling the right leg. The left arm hangs down, with its hand inclined partly under

the seat. The individual, who was a male, did not probably exceed the age of 14 at his death. There is a deep and extensive fracture of the skull, near the occiput, which probably killed him. The skin has sustained little injury; it is of a dusky color, but the natural hue cannot be decided with exactness, from its present appearance. The scalp, with small exceptions, is covered with sorrel or foxy hair. The teeth are white and sound. The hands and feet, in their shriveled state, are slender and delicate.[25]

In 1841, showman P.T. Barnum purchased the Scudder Museum and its contents. The name was changed to Barnum's American Museum. The exhibition of the mummified body contributed to Barnum's fame and fortune of the day. Thousands of visitors saw the body on display and in illustrations circulated in pamphlets published by Barnum. The museum and all its contents, mummy included, however, were destroyed in a catastrophic fire on July 13, 1865.[26]

The third mummified body from Short Cave became the most famous of the three, firmly placing Mammoth Cave in the public arena of tourism after the War of 1812. This was an adult female, buried beneath the floor of Short Cave, just beyond where the mummy of the infant was found. The rocks surrounding her body were later identified by archaeologists as forming a stone box grave, characteristic of the ancient Woodland Culture.

Like the other bodies, she was preserved by the dryness of the cave interior and contact with nitrates in the soil. Estimated to be in her late teens or early twenties when she died, her actual cause of death is unknown. A deep wound, however, was found in the back of her neck. This female mummy was originally displayed in Mammoth Cave just beyond the natural entrance in the Rotunda where one of the saltpeter mining operations was established.

Massachusetts antiquarian Nahum Ward read about the discovery and display of the mummy in the scientific journals of the day. Ward possessed a keen interest in the Indian mounds of Ohio. In 1815, he requested permission from cave manager Archibald Miller to view the mummy. Shortly after, he traveled to the cave accompanied by two guides.

Ward examined the remains of the dried-out human body in the Rotunda. Because of the seasonally damp conditions in this area of the cave, Ward suggested that the body be moved to a dry upper-level passage known as the Haunted Chambers. There she was displayed in a makeshift upright crypt on a stone ledge.[27]

Soon after his visit, Ward obtained ownership of the mummy. According to family correspondence, he believed it would be best to have the body preserved in a museum. Ward also wished to capitalize on the mummy's exhibition, but no verification has been found to substantiate his claim that he discovered the body.[28]

Ward published a map and an article concerning his visit in the *Worcester Spy*. He included an illustration of the mummy in which he added a human face to the skeletal body. This contributed greatly to the morbid desire of people to see this anthropological marvel.[29]

Ward then took the mummy on tour. For a fee, a curious person could see the Mammoth Cave Mummy, also referred to as the Queen of the Cave, in various cities and towns along his journey back to his native Massachusetts. Accounts describing her discovery and exhibition were published in American and European journals and newspapers. This sparked international interest in Mammoth Cave and its wonders.

After the War of 1812 ended, it was safe to travel again. Journeys by stagecoach to Mammoth Cave began in 1816. Tourists came to see the mummies and other curiosities on display. When the travelers arrived at the cave at great personal and financial expense, however, they discovered that there was no mummy to be seen. Instead, the guides began showing the limestone ledge in the Haunted Chambers where the female mummy had formerly been displayed. This Mummy Seat became a regular stopover on tours.

In 1814, a mummy was discovered in the Audubon Avenue section of Mammoth Cave by one of cave co-owner Charles Wilkins' workers. It was, however, re-buried under stones until 1840, at which time the new owner of the cave found it again while looking for the original location of the body. The weight of the stones covering the body had damaged the mummy so badly that it was not of display quality. Further information has not been found regarding the characteristics of the body or whether it was removed from the cave.[30]

Due to the popularity of the mummies on display, after the war was over Short Cave became known as a necropolis, or city of the dead. It was often referred to as Mummy Cave. In 1817, the American Antiquarian Society obtained the female body from Ward. In 1818, three mummies from the Mammoth Cave area were displayed in various cities, including Worcester, Massachusetts, New York City, and Cincinnati, Ohio.

Although she was no longer on display at Mammoth Cave, the stories of her discovery and exhibition were capitalized upon. Perhaps the most significant find was her necklace made of young deer hooves. In reference to this artifact, she was given the name Fawn Hoof, Kentucky's Posthumous Belle in 1853 by Nathaniel Parker Willis in his book, *A Health Trip to the Tropics.*[31]

Through the years, the legend of Fawn Hoof and the other Mammoth Cave mummies began to grow like fish tales. Successive guides would embellish the story to fit their own beliefs, superstitions, and interests. One version is that the Fawn Hoof mummy was found with the mummified body of a small child close to her in its own stone box grave. Subsequent stories are that the discovery of the bodies was made in Mammoth Cave itself, rather than Short Cave. This is the result of confusion between where the mummies were discovered and where they were exhibited after their exhumation. No doubt proprietary interests played a major role as well.

In his *A Guidebook to Mammoth Cave*, Dr. Charles W. Wright wrote of the mummies:

> They were both in a state of perfect preservation. There can be no doubt but they wandered into this avenue, and becoming bewildered, sat down, and died in the position in which they were found.[32]

In 1870, Dr. William Stump Forwood published *Mammoth Cave of Kentucky*, at the time the main publication on Mammoth Cave. He expressed doubts about the entire story of the discovery and placement of the mummies.[33]

Fawn Hoof was a fascinating, although morbid, display for various traveling shows and museums until she was acquired by the Smithsonian Institution's National Museum in 1876. Due to deterioration of her body, the flesh was removed around the turn of the century and the mummy was consigned to a box with an accession number.[34] Radiocarbon dating of her body in 1993 revealed that she died approximately 2,950 years ago. This former Queen of the Cave is still in the museum collection today, although not on display.[35]

After the Civil War, tourism began to hit its stride once more in the Mammoth Cave region. The finding of another mummy to bolster tourism became an urgent need for owners and proprietors of Mammoth Cave.

In 1875, such a mummy was found in Salts Cave, one of several caves owned by the proprietors of the Mammoth Cave estate. Salts Cave rivals Mammoth Cave in the size of its rooms. It was also a focal point of prehistoric mining of the cave minerals that give the cave its name. Local people believed that the two caves were linked together.

The mummified body discovered in Salts Cave was that of a child estimated to be about ten years of age at death. Although referred to as the Egyptian Mummy after its initial discovery, the most common name given to the child was Little Alice.

William Cutliff and Henry Lee were given credit for the discovery, although according to an early published interview with his daughter, Louis Vial was also involved as well. William Cutliff was hired by Vial to survey the property that Vial owned. Cutliff and Vial went on a trip through an entrance known only to themselves at the time. Each had balls of twine and oil lamps with extra bottles of oil. They unwound the twine until they got to the point where the body was discovered, today known as Mummy Valley. They found the mummy lying on a ledge on the wall of the cave, just above the floor of a narrow passage. There were piles of ashes and burnt sticks nearby. In the interview, "it was revealed that artifacts found with the mummy included a bowl, a pipe, several pairs of bark and grass moccasins (slippers) and the folded body estimated to be about 18 inches long."[36]

The body was removed from its resting place in the cave and was displayed at various commercial caves during the late 1800s and early 1900s.

The first known display of the child's body was by Larkin J. Proctor, a former manager of Mammoth Cave. He began showing it in his own cave, today known as Long Cave. The wooden mummy closet where the body of the child was placed is still intact in the cave, which is no longer shown to the public.

In the late 1800s, the child mummy was purchased by Henry Ganter, a stagecoach line operator and manager of the Mammoth Cave Hotel. It was then obtained by George Morrison who was owner of the New Entrance tours to Mammoth Cave during the period of 1921 to 1931. He had visited Ganter on one of his many excursions to the Mammoth Cave area between 1916 and 1920. He had examined the body of the child in the loft of Ganter's barn, where it had been stored for a number of years.

As the culmination of Morrison's tour through the more scenic Frozen Niagara portions of his cave, upon exiting the cave a visitor could see the child's body on display in a brass and glass coffin. This display of the dead was promoted as being the "Petrified Girl of Mammoth Cave—a little girl turned to stone, probably being captured by the Indians and died of fright."[37]

Little Alice was later found to be a male, and renamed Little Al. The mummy was the subject of scientific research in the early 1970s when a sample of tissue was obtained from the University of Kentucky Anthropology Department to be examined for red blood cells and possible diseases. The proceedings were presented at a symposium on skeletal biology in 1972, and published in *Science* the following year. These were the first published blood tests performed on a prehistoric mummy. Today the child mummy is preserved in a special container at the University of Kentucky in Lexington.[38]

The most famous display of the dead at Mammoth Cave in modern times came after the discovery of a mummified body of a male, estimated to be in his early forties at death. His post-mortem nickname was Lost John. He met his fate on a rock ledge, today called Mummy Ledge, nearly twenty feet above the present day tourist trail in Mammoth Cave.[39]

Lost John was removing mineral salts from the soils and walls of the cave ledge. In his zeal he dislodged a support stone holding a large boulder in place, which fell and crushed his body into the dry, nitrate-rich soil of the ledge. According to carbon 14 tests of the body, he met his demise around 2,000 years ago.

A curious coincidence is that Lost John was discovered by Grover Campbell and Lyman Cutliff, a descendant of William Cutliff, a discoverer of Little Al(ice).

Lost John was removed from display permanently in 1976. Due to desecration of burial sites throughout North America by grave robbers and pot hunters, Congress later passed legislation to prohibit public display of the physical remains of ancient North American peoples. Visitors who remember seeing Lost John still inquire about him today. In modern times, tours by the light of lanterns make a stop at Mummy Ledge, while National Park Service guides recount the story of his discovery and exhibition.

In an interview, a resident of the Mammoth Cave area during the turn of the century stated that human bones were often dug up out of caves in the region. In one case, a human skull was on exhibit in the lobby of a former hotel in the nearby town of Cave City.[40]

Fantastic tales were told of bodies being found that conjured up images of a vanished race. The "bones of a giant bereft of its head by a fearless antiquary" is referred to in one of the most popular guidebooks, *Rambles in the Mammoth Cave*, published in 1845.[41]

Today, visitors who are curious about these former displays of the dead must be content with the stories told by park guides, published materials on sale at the park bookstore, and by the thought that other remains may be hidden in the caves below.

GHOSTS

No scary place worth its salt would be without ghost stories, and Mammoth Cave has its share, both old and new. Your odds of meeting ghosts in Mammoth Cave are slim, but modern visitors do occasionally see an apparition first met in the early 1880s by cave guide William Garvin. William was walking along the cave passage called Broadway when the glowing figure of a woman floating in the air above the trail appeared before him. After a few minutes the ghost faded into the darkness. William proceeded toward the place where the ghost had been, ready with his cane raised to chase the spirit away in case it took a notion to pull any tricks. Although he thought he was the only living soul in the cave, he soon met a party of tourists coming down the passage. He realized that the ghostly figure he had seen was merely the glow from a Bengal light, (a flare used to light the cave in the days before electric lights) shining through the curved rocks along the passage.[42] This ghost is today known as Martha Washington's Statue and is sometimes seen on the Historic Tour, where a flick of a switch turns on electric lights to recreate the illusion that spooked Mr. Garvin more than a century ago.

———————

One writer apparently inspired by the mystery and spookiness of Mammoth Cave was a nineteenth century author Nathan Ryno Smith. In 1869, his "Legend of Mammoth Cave" was featured in his book *Legends of the South*. Smith's legend, a product of his own imagination, is the story of a curious traveler who arrived at Mammoth Cave in search of local lore. He met a man who told him of an Indian who many years earlier visited the cave once a year to spend twenty-four hours underground. When the Indian was a child, his people were surrounded by the white man in battle. Rather than die at enemy hands, they entered Mammoth Cave, where they perished, causing the child to be the last of his tribe. Upon the Indian's last visit to the cave he told the man he was:

> . . . determined to enter and explore these
> awful chambers . . . . What I have there
> discovered, the Great Spirit forbids me to
> reveal.
> This is the last visit that I shall ever
> make to the tomb of my tribe. I shall enter
> and you will see me no more.

Hearing this story sparked the traveler's curiosity, so he hired a guide and descended into the cave to explore. He left his guide and met the spirit of the Indian, who took him to the final resting place of his tribe. He gave the traveler a premonition of the consequences the white man would face for his evil deeds against the Indians.

> We were hunted from hill to hill, from
> valley to valley, like those beasts of prey,

William Garvin meets a "Ghost."

the wolf and the panther. Do you not
know, pale face, that your people are now
engaged in exterminating the last remnant
of our race? The warrior, the squaw and
the papoose, are alike the victims of their
rapacious cruelty.

Will the Great Spirit forever delay? No!
I foresee the approach of the avenger. . . .

The bear of the North shall wage war
with the panther of the South, and terrible
shall be the conflict.[43]

After hearing the prophecy (referring to the Civil
War), the traveler fell asleep. Upon awakening he was
unaware of how long he has been underground. He
quickly made his way back to the subterranean river
where he found his guide anxiously awaiting his return.

The colorful nineteenth century ghosts in these
stories are all the result of imagination or some ex-
plainable event. Today's spooks are more serious about
their craft! Modern visitors cannot always explain the
strange things they see or feel.

As you stroll along a huge passage called Main Cave,
you see why this is called the Historic Tour; old wooden
water pipes, beams, and vats the saltpeter miners used in
the early 1800s lie beside the trail. Some pipes are still
propped up on stones where the miners left them on
their last day on the job. The miners reportedly used this
area for church services,[44] giving the room its name: the
Methodist Church.

Blackouts are popular at the Church during cave
tours. One guide turns out the lights, while the other
guide speaks to the visitors on the opposite side of the
room, sometimes by lantern light. Cave guide Larry
Pursell was walking from the tour group to the light
switch one day when he saw a family in the cave.

The cave was now lit by the lard oil lamp. . .
About half way back to the light switch I
noticed a black family standing 10 to 20 feet
to the rear of the group. There was a man,
his wife and a son and daughter, each wearing black and white apparel. The father also
wore a white Panama hat. I didn't recall any
such family at the gate, but I really wasn't
paying attention to who had entered the
cave on our trip. My thought was that they
were from the Caribbean area and perhaps
did not speak English. I altered my path a
little so that I might invite them to join the
group. I got to within just a few feet of
them, close enough to see facial details. I
was about to speak when I noticed they
were very intent on watching Gary, so I just
veered back toward the light switch, not
wanting to spoil their experience.

Just about the time I got to the light
switch, Gary asked for the lights. As I
pushed the "on" button . . . [the family] was
not there! I searched the entire group as
they passed me. Not a single black person
was on that trip! The family I had gotten
within six feet of had vanished!

I said nothing to Gary until we returned
to the guide lounge after the trip. I pulled
him aside and asked him if he'd seen a black
family on our trip. He said, "No, why?"
With a little trepidation I began to recount
the story. . . . Someone half jokingly quip-
ped, "Well Larry, that was one of the old
slave guides and his family!" [Most of the
guides at Mammoth Cave in the mid-1800s
were slaves.] As I mulled the incident over
in my mind, I began to think about those

old Sunday morning services in the cave. Surely a guide would have assisted the minister in moving the congregation to the Methodist Church area. If his family had joined him, they would have stood back away from the rest of the group, as would have been required by the custom of the day.

Was there a family standing respectfully in the rear on a Sunday morning visit to Mammoth Cave, as they had done 140 years ago? I do not know. They were as real to me as any other person standing six feet away in the twilight. I have visited the cave many other times, recreating that trip. Using lanterns, torches, flashlights, and carbide lamps, I have not been able to recreate even the faintest resemblance of that family. There is nothing on that part of the trail to reflect light in such a fashion to be misconstrued as a man wearing a white vest and Panama hat, much less his wife and two children! . . . You decide who I saw![45]

Cave guide Joy Lyons reported a different kind of meeting at the Church during a blackout.

All of a sudden I felt a very strong, firm push to my right shoulder, it was like a shove, a playful shove. It was hard enough that I stepped forward. I said, "Cut it out," because I thought it was David. About the time I said, "Cut it out," Red [David and Red were other guides] lit his lantern and I could see David very obviously silhouetted to the right of the group, he had walked up in the darkness and was standing by the group. I wouldn't say I panicked, but I was definitely upset. I committed the big sin of turning on my flashlight and flashed it everywhere. There was no one behind me, no one on the dirt piles, no one on the hill. This all happened in a couple of seconds, there was no time for anyone to have gone very far. . . .

I still ponder it to this day; it was a very real thing I experienced. . . . My mind is wide open, it could have been a lot of things, but I always had the feeling it was someone trying to get my attention.[46]

Kerry Woods, another National Park Service guide, had a similar experience at the Church.

We were the first tour to enter the cave at the Methodist Church. While I was at the light switch I heard footsteps coming toward me from Booth's Amphitheater [a cave room near Methodist Church]. I tried to ignore it, but it kept getting closer. Then I got shoved on my right shoulder. As I looked back no one was there, at least no one I could see.[47]

According to some accounts, pushy ghosts do not attend church every day. Another favorite haunt is near the end of the Historic Tour, where a small, dark passage called Little Bat Avenue intersects with the huge, brightly-lit Audubon Avenue. Guide Neila Spradlin gives this account.

When we arrived at the light switch between Little Bat and Audubon, the guide had me turn off the lights. I kept my hand

on top of the switch and felt a touch on it.
It was enough to move my hand! It was not
a bat; it felt like a hand! I abruptly shined
my flashlight all around, but the group was
at least five feet ahead of me and no one
was behind or beside me.[48]

At the same switch, on a different trip, guide Jaime
Gray had a similar experience.

I was by the light switch in Little Bat. I
am standing in the darkness waiting to hear
the key phrase to hit the lights back on
when all of a sudden a hand reached and
grabbed my left forearm. . . . I immediately
turned the light on and no one was any-
where around.[49]

On the Historic route in the cave, one at least has the
option of electric lights. The cave is a little less mysterious and spooky once the switch is flipped on. But that
twentieth century luxury runs out as you continue along
Main Cave. You step back into the Mammoth Cave of the
nineteenth century. The Violet City Lantern Tour goes on
with the aid of glowing lanterns. This atmosphere seems
perfect for strange happenings. It was on this tour that
National Park Service guide Charles Hanion had this
experience in a huge room called Chief City:

A lady said, "Who is that up there
among the rocks?" We thought somebody
had gotten off trail, but the pile of rocks was
very huge, it was very hard to get off trail in
that part of the cave. I looked where the
lady had pointed; Steve [another guide]
turned around and looked. It looked like
somebody was actually standing up on

Sacrifice Rock. You couldn't make out many details, but it looked like someone with a long sleeved shirt, probably white, wearing a hat, the old droop style hat some of the early slave guides had worn in the cave. . . . It also looked like the person was holding a lantern. . . . Because Steve had lit up the rock [by throwing a torch] we thought it had created a series of shadows. The only thing is, it had a dimensional look to it, because it was seen from three different angles, like you could see an actual person standing there. We had a good laugh and went on with the rest of the trip.

It was the next trip that made things stick out in my mind all these years. . . . What a lady asked me was, "Have you ever had people in this part of the cave who shouldn't be here?" I said, "What are you talking about?" She said, "People who are from another time or place." We hadn't been talking about ghosts or anything like that on the trip. She was very spooked for the rest of her journey. She claimed to be a psychic, so that might have had something to do with it. For the rest of the trip she claimed that she wanted to get out of the cave because that was a spooky experience.

On another Violet City Lantern trip, Charles knew he would meet members of the volunteer organization Earthwatch who were in the passage cataloging artifacts that day. As he rounded a bend he was startled to see a group of coverall suited people sitting and leaning on the rocks. He did not expect to see the volunteers so soon. He approached the person closest to the trail to chastise him for scaring the daylights out of him. As the lantern behind Charlie better lit the scene, the image disappeared! The Earthwatch workers were further down the passage where they were expected to be.[50]

Continue along the lantern lit trail on your Violet City trek and you soon find yourself at Mummy Ledge, where Mammoth Cave employees Lyman Cutliff and Grover Campbell made the amazing find that gave the room its name in 1935. Cutliff's son, Park Service veteran Lewis Cutliff, tells his father's story of the discovery and the unusual experience his father and Cambell had soon after.

Daddy explored the caves since he was little. He'd just go with his daddy and they would find things in Salts Cave. He would see the same type of things in Mammoth Cave. He knew that his Uncle Bill Cutliff had found a mummy in Salts Cave, so he and Grover started looking around. They decided if there was one in Salts Cave there might be one in Mammoth Cave.

Daddy was off one day and Grover had been in the cave the night before by himself with his crew. The next day he had daddy come up on a ledge. He wanted to show him something he'd found the day before, some mummified bats. They crawled around this boulder and Grover put his hand down. It felt funny. He cursed, came out with an oath, and said, "What is that?" He moved back and Daddy came and looked at it and said, "Well Grover, that's what we've been looking for, that's a mummy's head. . . .

After Grover and Daddy found it they had to stay in the cave and guard it at night.

43

While they were there they looked around.
They went to a passage called Blue Springs
Branch and were digging around. Grover
put his hand down a hole and was digging
around when they heard three knocks. It
scared Grover. . . . Daddy said, "Let me put
my hand down there." . . . He heard three
knocks and three more knocks, like somebody hit a rock on another rock. It frightened both of them; it was loud enough that
they heard it! So they went back up and
stayed where the mummy was. He was
never able to explain it, but it seemed like
anything that happened to either one of
them was always in threes, three knocks, you
know, and three more. Grover died three
years later. It was six years after that Daddy
lost his job. It was thirty years later my sister
had open-heart surgery and then she died in
three years. He always felt like he shouldn't
have bothered the mummy, he just felt
that's what caused all the problems they had.
He often said if he had it to do over again
that he'd never tell it.[51]

Unexplainable sounds disrupted caver Michael Nardacci and his research companion on a peaceful lunch
break. They accompanied two paleontologists and a
photographer into Marion Avenue, a cave passage near
the Snowball Dining Room, the lunch stop for visitors on
the Grand Avenue tour. Michael and his companion
separated from the scientists to do historic research.
Michael returned to the surface with this story.

People who have never been in a cave
passage—particularly a truly quiet one like

44

Marion Avenue, so far above Mammoth's noisy base-level passages—cannot begin to conceive of what the term "silence" means . . . the silence seemed to engulf us. It is an unnerving awareness, and while caving I frequently will make some noise, no matter how unnecessary or redundant, to break that silence. I had just finished a can of fruit cocktail and a Heath bar and was washing it down with a gulp from my canteen, when suddenly from just around a bend in the passage ahead of us came heart-stopping sounds: **Bang! Bang!** The air reverberated—perhaps the walls did, too. . . .

"What the hell was that?" we said in tandem; if we had rehearsed it we could not have spoken the words together more precisely.

Understand: this noise was not produced by a couple of rocks suddenly falling from the ceiling. . . . We know this because in the numbing few minutes after hearing the sounds we experimented with different shapes and sizes of rocks dropped from varying heights onto packed sediment or bedrock. The sounds we had heard were *bangs:* concentrated, powerful, suggestive of purpose—and perhaps of fury.

. . . Of course, we mulled over the possibility that the trio who we had escorted into the side passage was playing a joke on the two guys who had accompanied them into the cave and who might be feeling a little creepy being so isolated. But it was over an hour before they returned, breathing hard, muddied up and complaining of the tightness of the passage they had to follow. It would be unreasonable to assume that they had sat there in contorted positions for better than sixty minutes to see the effect that their little joke had on two men in a remote section of the world's longest cave. In any event they apparently had not heard the sounds; they did not mention them, we surely did not. . . .

For several years after the event . . . whenever we would meet at CRF [Cave Research Foundation] expeditions, one of us would invariably greet the other by saying, "I didn't hear anything that day. Did you?" And the other would echo, "Nope, not a thing!"[52]

Some accounts have a different twist. Mammoth Cave guide Sarah Flowers reported seeing the ghost of guide Kathy Proffitt. This was not your typical ghost, since Kathy was alive and well. Sarah was in a cave room called Great Relief Hall waiting for people on the Historic Tour to pop out of the appropriately named passage, Fat Man's Misery. When she saw her partner Kathy come out of the hole, she knew everyone had arrived, so she turned out the lights in Fat Man's Misery. A couple of minutes later Kathy stepped out of the dark passage, flashlight in hand. This was a surprise, since several people had thought she was already there. No one else in the group was wearing what resembled a Park Service uniform.[53] Everyone's eyes playing tricks at once?

When you are out of the cave and back on the surface world, you may not want to breathe a sigh of relief too quickly. A strange sight reported by Joy Medley Lyons suggests that cave ghosts may even occasionally come above ground to get a little sun now and then.

One afternoon Cris [another park employee] and I were walking across the footbridge to the hotel. . . . It was mid-afternoon and the shadows were just right, it could have been shadows. We both saw, at least I saw, two sets of legs from just above the knee down walking down over the grassy bank. It startled me, I stopped walking and Cris stopped too. She looked over at me and I said, "Did you see that?" She said, "Two of them, right?" I said, "Yeah." We shook our heads and kept walking. It was the weirdest thing."[54]

An old View Master reel shows people without upper bodies walking through the Snowball Dining Room inside Mammoth Cave. This photographic mistake makes it appear that ghostly legs like to grab lunch after their jaunts to the surface!

Many others have experienced strange things underground such as hearing voices or seeing people when no one is around. Many have also heard or seen people who turn out to be maintenance people, or other workers around the corner. Which are you hearing?

FLOYD

$\mathbf{F}$ew people in history are elevated to the status of being remembered primarily by their first names: Jesus, Napoleon, Floyd. What!? You don't know Floyd? Then I must tell you his story and why cavers know him so well.

The section of the Mammoth Cave System where cavers most often encounter the unexplainable is Floyd Collins' Crystal Cave. Crystal Cave was connected to Mammoth Cave in September, 1972. The connection between the Flint Ridge Cave System (which Crystal Cave is a part of) and the Mammoth Cave System made Mammoth Cave part of the world's longest known cave system.[55] It is little wonder that those who enter Crystal Cave get the shivers, because for many years the cave was the resting place of the body of the famous caver Floyd Collins who died in 1925. Until Crystal Cave was closed to the public in 1961, tourists could pay Floyd a post-mortem visit, and cave researchers continued to walk by his underground casket until he was reburied in 1989.[56] Knowing that there was a dead man in the cave for more than sixty years may give you an idea of why going into Crystal Cave could be a spooky experience, but one cannot truly appreciate Floyd and his after death antics unless one knows the whole story.

Floyd Collins, like many people around Mammoth Cave, had a passion for caves. And like many people around Mammoth Cave, he had a passion for making money from caves. Floyd and his family guided tours in Crystal Cave and sold artifacts found underground, but Floyd wanted in on the real action.

Since the early 1800s, there have been guided tours through the caves of south central Kentucky. By the beginning of the twentieth century the increased competition for the tourist dollar led to cave wars between commercial caves. Show-cave employees would dress like police officers and stand at information booths along the road to stop travelers bound for Mammoth Cave. In the quest for more customers, these solicitors did their best to direct tourists to their employers' caves.

The Collins family was losing the cave wars. Crystal was a beautiful cave, but was farther off the beaten path than the other show caves. It was on a rough dirt road and offered no modern accommodations for travelers. Floyd knew a better location was needed to attract tourists. He knew of a cave called Sand Cave along the main highway leading to Mammoth Cave. He knew that by stopping tourists on their way to Mammoth, he would get plenty of business if Sand Cave was of show quality. So Floyd set out to explore Sand Cave.

Although he was an experienced caver, Floyd often broke one of the most important rules of caving—never cave alone. If you run into trouble there is no one to help you or to get help. On January 30, 1925, while exploring Sand Cave alone, a twenty-five pound rock[57] slipped and caught Floyd's foot, trapping him in the narrow passage with no one to hear his calls for help.

Floyd was missed the next day. Friends went to Sand Cave, fearing the worst. They called down into the cave and heard Floyd yell back, "Come to me, I'm hung up." He asked them to send for his brother Homer and his friend Johnny Gerald, a caving companion who had freed him when he had once been stuck in Crystal Cave.

Family and friends were soon there. Those who were small enough and brave enough could actually crawl down to Floyd and feed him while they worked on freeing him from his underground prison.

What began as a local cave rescue quickly erupted into much more. Newspapers soon got word of the event. Radio stations and motion picture companies heard as well. As the nation learned of Floyd's plight, they wanted daily updates on the rescue attempt. People were snapping up papers as soon as they hit the newsstand, causing huge numbers of extra editions to be printed. To hear about Floyd, listeners tuned their radios to special broadcasts that interrupted regular programming. Silent movie theaters featured newsreels showing rescuers at work.

When the media ran out of fresh news, they turned to whatever colorful stories they could come up with. Reporters wrote of Floyd's sweetheart, who stood by the cave entrance calling to her lover, and Floyd's faithful dog, who refused to eat or leave the cave entrance until his master was safe. It was beside the point that Floyd showed little interest in women and the family dog probably did not know that Floyd was trapped.

All the publicity brought plenty of curious people to Sand Cave. So many arrived on the weekend that the atmosphere of Sand Cave was like a carnival. The country road leading to the rescue site was choked bumper to bumper with cars and horse-drawn vehicles. The L&N Railroad added extra coaches to its Louisville to Cave City train. Stands selling hot dogs and hamburgers were set up to feed the crowds. Booths were set up to sell cave onyx, heal-all elixirs, moonshine, and balloons with SAND CAVE printed on them. The rescue scene was so macabre that it eventually inspired the movie

Ace in the Hole staring Kirk Douglas, about the carnival scene that sprang up when a man was trapped in a mine.

About the fifth day of Floyd's entrapment, a rock fall possibly occurred in Sand Cave. Rescue workers stopped crawling all the way to Floyd, although they could hear his voice awhile longer. They decided to dig a shaft to get to him, since rescuing him through the natural passage seemed impossible.

More than two weeks after the ordeal began, the shaft reached Floyd. A rescue worker scrambled down to him, but Floyd was dead. The sad, but unsurprising information was quickly relayed to the Collins family and the rest of the country, who had adopted Floyd as their own. Floyd's body remained in the cave for two and a half months before being brought out through a second shaft. He was buried on Collins family land near Crystal Cave.

After a couple of years at rest, Floyd had to make another move. His father, Lee Collins, sold Crystal Cave to Dr. H. B. Thomas, a local dentist already in the commercial cave business. With the purchase, Dr. Thomas obtained permission to move Floyd's body into Crystal Cave for display in a glass topped coffin. His facial features were restored by a mortician to make him presentable. Floyd was more successful attracting customers to Crystal Cave after his death than he was in life.

Two years into his stint as a tourist attraction, Floyd's body was abducted. The body (supposedly minus the left leg) was soon found near the Green River. Perhaps owners of rival caves felt that getting rid of Floyd would lessen competition from Crystal Cave. Or had Dr. Thomas arranged the theft knowing it would bring publicity to Crystal Cave?

After most of Floyd was recovered and returned, Dr. Thomas replaced the coffin's glass lid with a regular coffin lid. This did not stop visitors from lifting the lid to take an occasional peek at Floyd.

In 1961, the National Park Service purchased Crystal Cave and public tours ended. Floyd stayed in his subterranean repose with only occasional visits from cavers, researchers, and park staff until he was moved to the Mammoth Cave Baptist Church Cemetery in 1989. For more details about Floyd Collins, see the book *Trapped!* by Robert Murray and Roger Brucker.[58]

Unusual experiences in Crystal Cave have caused many people to wonder if Floyd was not content just to lie around after he was put to rest in the cave.

In 1954, the Collins' Crystal Cave expedition (C-3 for short) was conducted to explore Crystal Cave. Cavers Roy Charlton, Roger McClure, and Roger Brucker were exploring far back in the cave when they heard a voice call, "Wait!" The cavers stopped, thinking someone else from the expedition might be trying to join them. Several minutes passed and nothing else was heard. They laughingly attributed the voice to the little men, the imaginary little people cavers sometimes blame strange noises on. They concluded that another party must have been working in the same part of the cave. Upon returning to the base camp they checked the logbook to see if any other cavers had been in that area. The eerie feeling they had felt earlier returned when the cavers learned that no other parties had been in that part of the cave.

Other members of the C-3 expedition also heard voices in the cave. Joe Lawrence said he and his companion waited half an hour for someone to catch up when they heard people talking in the distance, but nobody came.[59] Unexplainable noises and sightings have long been part of caving. If little men are not at fault, mythical cave creatures called hodags often take the blame.

According to the stories, Floyd has a wide repertoire of tricks to draw from. Some people say if Floyd has nothing to say he will get your attention another way!

In the early 1970s, some National Park Service employees were on a trip in Crystal Cave. Most of the party went beyond Floyd's resting place to see the gypsum formations that cover Crystal's walls. Park rangers Robert and Zona Cetera stayed near the casket to photograph it. While setting off a flash, Bob heard footsteps in the gravel. Zona, who was standing by the camera across the room, heard it too. When the rest of the party returned about an hour later, they told the Ceteras nobody had left the group. The footsteps came from the side of the room opposite the passage the party had taken, so if someone had sneaked off to play a joke, Bob and Zona would have seen them cross the room.[60]

While taking a cave class, caver Candice Leek was moving through a rough, rocky section of Unknown-Crystal Cave when she tripped and began to fall into a five-foot-deep canyon. She knew bones would break when she hit bottom. Then:

> Suddenly, a strong hand grabbed me
> from behind on my right upper arm. After
> I regained my balance I turned and said,
> "Thank you, Richard," [another caver] but
> no one was there! Richard was on the
> other side of the passage. I wonder if
> Floyd saved me? I uttered a quick, "Thank
> you, Floyd," and left the cave.[61]

On a training trip into Crystal Cave in 1987, a party of National Park Service employees walked through a dirt passage Floyd and his brothers had excavated just beyond the casket containing Floyd's body. On the return trip through the passage, a sound like someone flipping his fingers on a drinking glass caused ranger Charles Hanion to look to see what it was. At that time he noticed an old whiskey bottle, perched on one of the sandy shelves of the passage, begin to move outward from the wall and drop down in front of him as he was walking. He gave an accusatory laugh directed toward the members of the group walking in front of him and said, "Who did that?!" But denials came from all around. Nobody ever admitted to rigging the bottle to fall.[62]

An old whiskey bottle is not the only thing cavers have reported hearing Floyd ring. Will White tells about an experience he and fellow researcher George Deike had in Crystal Cave.

> The date was July 22, 1961. That much is certain because it was recorded in my field notebook. George Deike and I were on our way to Lost Passage, me to collect data on breakdown and George to collect data for his dissertation. We were just beginning to descend into Grand Canyon when there came a ringing sound. I looked at George to see if he had maybe banged his carbide lamp against the steel handrail of the old tourist trail. He was looking at me wondering the same thing. Then the ringing sound came again, definitely from the darkness at the bottom of the canyon. It was one of those moments. We had to know what it was and we both started running down the trail toward the sound. A few moments later we were standing between the coffin and the telephone. The ringing sound came a third time. We were immensely relieved to find that the sound came from the telephone and not from the coffin.

I picked up the phone. It was the old army type with a butterfly switch to talk. What I heard in the receiver was what you hear when you hear when someone you've called lays down the phone to go get something but there are other people in the room. You hear noises from the room and scraps of background conversation, but generally can't made out much of what is being said. So I clicked the switch and said, "Hello, is someone trying to call Crystal Cave?" Then there was a sound like someone has picked up the receiver on the other end. So I said again, "Hello, is someone trying call Crystal Cave?" There was a startled gasp and the line went dead.

There was no further response from the telephone (or the coffin), so we continued on to Lost Passage to do our fieldwork. Some hours later we returned, walking down Dyer Avenue, approaching the coffin with some trepidation. All was silent. . . .

On the way out of the cave we traced the phone wires back to the entrance and up the hill toward the old ticket office. Near the ticket office the cut ends of the line were dangling from a pole with no further connection to anything.[63]

One account makes it appear that Floyd has not limited his activities to inside the cave. George Wood and a companion were checking springs as part of a ground water study in June, 1976. The last on their list was Pike Spring near Crystal Cave. While sitting and enjoying the quiet of the evening in a truck awaiting his

Will White gets a Crystal Cave phone call.

partner's return from the spring, George had an experience worth telling:

> My reverie was broken by a man
> shouting in the distance. At first I thought
> it was Bill calling for help, but the voice
> wasn't pitched low enough. The sound was
> so faint that I had to listen carefully in or-
> der to understand what was being said.
> Whoever it was cried, "Help! Help me,
> I'm trapped. Johnnie help me!" over and
> over again.
> That shook me!

George's partner soon returned.

> As we were driving home I asked him
> if he had heard any shouting. He replied
> that he hadn't. I then told him what had
> happened. He asked me if I had known
> that Floyd was buried in Crystal Cave just
> down the hill from where we parked. I
> hadn't. We were both a little spooked then
> and Bill entertained me the rest of the way
> home with Floyd Collins ghost stories. A
> few months later, a co-worker heard the
> story and decided to do some checking on
> "Johnnie." We expected him to find sev-
> eral Johnnies that Floyd had known. He
> found only one, John "Johnnie" Gerald, a
> good friend of Floyd's, one of many peo-
> ple who tried to rescue Collins from Sand
> Cave, and one of the last to talk with him
> before a ceiling collapse sealed him off
> from any rescue attempts. Floyd Collins
> died shortly after the collapse, alone in the
> dark and the cold. Did I hear Floyd's ghost

crying out, or was it my imagination? I
don't know, I can only wonder.[64]

Of course, knowing you are sharing your underground space with a dead man can get the old imagination going and cause you to hear or see things that in a
less spooky place you would dismiss as nothing. Most
people (including those mentioned in this book) who
have entered Crystal Cave since the 1960s are people
seriously interested in caves who are not looking for
scary or weird things to occur. But unusual things can
happen even when your mind is on other business.

Geologists Art and Peg Palmer have spent many
years doing research and exploring in hundreds of
caves throughout the world. Usually they return to the
surface with the information they expected to find.
Crystal is the one cave that has also given them the
unexpected. Here Art Palmer tells of two unusual
experiences:

> The two of us were in the upper (southern)
> end of the Lost Passage on a lengthy photo
> trip. I was setting up for a sensuous por-
> trayal of chert nodules, when I became
> aware of a rhythmic pounding from down
> the passage. It was intense, but muffled, as
> though someone were beating vigorously
> with a hammer on a slab of rock about 500
> feet away. Eventually Peg looked up and
> asked, "What's that noise?" Naturally I
> played dumb and said, "What noise?" and
> then, "Oh that? It's just the reverberation
> of our heartbeats in this domed part of the
> ceiling. . . ."
>
> Nice try! The noise was as regular as the
> beat of a metronome, with individual
> strokes about a second apart, and clearly

coming from down the passage. This was not the random noise produced by rocks shifting, bats fluttering, or other natural causes of "ghostly" phenomena. How about dripping water? Not only is this section of passage perfectly dry, but drips produce high-frequency sounds that dissipate rapidly over short distances. They certainly could not produce the low, doom-laden tones that filled the air. (Sorry, I'm getting carried away with the spirit of the thing—although that may not be the proper word to use.) We decided it was time to shift our activities to a different part of the cave. Ironically, that meant heading toward the sound. But as we drew near to the apparent source, the sound faded away.

The overlaying land is uninhabited and there are no roads. There is no machinery in the area, and no one else had access to the cave that week. Few people knew how to get to that part of the cave, and none of them were within 100 miles of the cave that day. In unrelated seismic studies we've found that intense sledgehammer blows and truck traffic over 6-inch barriers at the surface cannot be detected in underlying caves without sensitive instruments, even as shallow as a few tens of meters. So what caused the noise?

Years later it dawned on us that the sound appeared to emanate from the very spot where Floyd Collins had set up a small camp and occasionally paused to eat, and where he would flatten his bean cans with a rock. (An insidious grin spreads across my face. . . .)

Here is Art's second story:

In 1969 three of us witnessed a bizarre
event in Collins Avenue. Peg and I were
taking photos near the cave entrance while
an off-duty ranger descended into the
Grand Canyon to photograph Floyd's
tomb (again note the photographic asso-
ciation.) Suddenly the ranger came huffing
up and gasped, "Did you hear that noise??"
No, we hadn't. So we all headed to the
Grand Canyon and were transfixed by the
loud beating of wings traveling back and
forth along the length of the room near
ceiling level. Evidently a large bird had
entered the cave and was seeking a way
out.

The noise was loud and intense, as
though we were standing beneath a bridge
with a train passing over it (well, not quite
that loud), and with distinct powerful
wing-beats. This was one big bird—maybe
a huge owl or wild turkey. A bat, you say?
Not a chance. Even the largest bats make
only faint fluttering noises reminiscent of a
butterfly on steroids. Strangely, with our
carbide and electric lamps going full blast
we could see nothing, even where the
sound appeared to be less than 20 feet
overhead. Another oddity is that the sound
moved rather slowly, about the speed of a
fast walk. We listened to it come and go
about ten times, then continued on into
the cave. We did not hear it on our way
out a couple of hours later. . . .

As time went on, the improbability
factor began to creep in. The hole in the

entrance gate at that time was barely large enough to admit a hand, and although a pigeon could be stuffed into it, the large bird in question would be unable (and probably unwilling) to squeeze through.

Moreover, our geologic surveying has brought us over every part of the Grand Canyon, and we have never found the slightest evidence for a bird—no droppings, feathers, or bones. . . .

Art Palmer reflects the feelings of many others that hear and see the unexplainable in Crystal and the rest of the Mammoth Cave System.

Have we renounced science and become ghost hunters? Naw. There must be a rational explanation for these sounds. . . .

What perks us up is that these, and many other strange phenomena in Crystal Cave reported by others, are still unexplained. We may never know what caused them, and in some ways I hope we do not. . . .

Scientists are always looking for answers, and yet sometimes when an answer is finally found, much of the excitement disappears.[65]

HELLISH NAMES

People of many cultures have believed that the world of the dead—Hell, or Hades—is located deep within the bowels of the Earth. It is little wonder then, that subterranean passages conjure up ideas of meeting the Devil himself. Some of Mammoth Cave's place names (with the year of the earliest known reference included)[66] reveal the feelings of early cave explorers and visitors.

Haunted Room–1811

Above the old saltpeter mining artifacts in the cavernous passage of Broadway, you look up into a passage called Gothic Avenue. This was once known as the Haunted Room, one of the oldest place names in Mammoth Cave.

There are several stories about how this avenue acquired its frightful name. In a 1920 interview, a local resident said that during the saltpeter mining operation of the early 1800s "a fellow got left behind, and as he came up on the rear of the Negroes they took him for a haunt and ran off from their work."[67] Mariam Ebenezer in an 1844 article in the *New York Municipal Gazette* states, "In some parts of the haunted room there is much echo from sound, a voice or sound is reverberated, and this gave the apartment the startling name." Ebenezer also mentions stalagmites that look like human figures standing in the darkness.[68] The best known explanation for the name is possibly fact with a little fiction thrown in. The story is that while mining saltpeter to make gunpowder in the early 1800s, a new and inexperienced miner was sent down a cave passage to get a few sacks of nitrous earth. The miner had been in the passage only once before, but had little worry of getting lost, since this section of cave has no side avenues in which to lose one's way. But on his return, he did not recall the trip being so long and began to fear he was in the wrong passage. In his panic he began to run, tripped and fell over a rock, putting out his lantern.

Thus left in the dark, not knowing where to turn, frightened out of his wits besides, he fell to remembering his sins—always remembered by those who are lost in the Cave—and praying with all his might for succor. But the hours passed away, and assistance came not; the poor fellow's frenzy increased; he felt himself a doomed man; he thought his terrible situation was a judgment imposed on him for his wickedness; nay, he even believed, at last, that he was no longer an inhabitant of the earth—that he had been translated, even in the body, to the place of torment—in other words, that he was in hell.

Fellow miners with glowing torches in hand finally arrived. But the frightened miner:

A lost miner sees glowing "eyes" in the
bowels of the earth.

. . . not doubting they were those identical devils whose appearance he had been expecting, took to his heels, yelling lustily for mercy; he did not stop, not withstanding the calls of his amazed friends, until he had fallen a second time over the rocks, where he lay on his face, roaring for pity,—until, by dint of much pulling and shaking, he was convinced that he was still in the world and the Mammoth Cave.[69]

Devil's Armchair–1827

In Gothic Avenue sits an odd shaped column formation that opens in the center to form a rather gruesome looking natural chair. It has been called Jenny Lind's Armchair, after a famous nineteenth century singer who according to a myth sat in it once while singing; and Wilkins' Armchair, after Charles Wilkins, an early 1800s cave owner. But the Devil's Armchair is the ghastly chair's most enduring name, perhaps because the Devil is more famous than Jenny Lind or Charles Wilkins.

Dante's Gateway–1897

Along Broadway looms an immense casket-shaped boulder appropriately named Giant's Coffin. As you step around the Coffin, the cave walls and ceiling that were so far apart just seconds ago begin to close in around you as you descend into the lower depths of the cave. This is Dante's Gateway. The name was inspired by Dante Alighieri's fourteenth century epic *The Divine Comedy,* in which he describes his visits to Heaven and Hell. According to this classic, over Hell's gate hangs a sign reading "All hope abandon, ye who enter here."[70] Did Mammoth Cave's nineteenth century visitors feel they were passing the point of no return?

The Bottomless Pit–1834

Imagine yourself in the 1830s. As you wind your

way through the labyrinth of Mammoth Cave, every-thing beyond the few feet of your flickering lantern light is a mystery. The guide says, "The ceiling is 300 feet high!" It may be so because it is so high you cannot see it. You come to a gaping pit. He proclaims, "It's bottomless!" That cannot be true, but you have little room to argue because the light from your lantern does not reach the bottom.

The name of this 105-foot-deep pit along the His-toric Tour route was inspired by another Bottomless Pit, mentioned in the Bible.

> And the fifth angel . . . opened the shaft of
> the Bottomless Pit, and from the shaft rose
> a smoke out of the pit, like the smoke of a
> great furnace, and the sun and the air were
> darkened from the smoke of the shaft.
> Revelation 9: 1-2.[71]

River Styx–1841

You are crossing the River Styx deep within the Earth in a world void of light and with little color. You might be entering Hades, the world of the dead in Greek mythology, or you may be just in Mammoth Cave. One 1800s cave visitor apparently felt the two locations were alike. He said that "The first glimpse of it [River Styx] brings to mind the descent of Ulysses into Hell."[72]

Charon's Cascade–1907

If you were in Hades on the bank of River Styx, you would make acquaintance with Charon, the boatman. His job is to ferry the souls of the dead into Hades for the fee of one coin. It was an ancient Greek custom to place a coin in the mouth of a corpse at burial so pay-ment could be made upon arrival.[73] Those who did not receive a proper burial, and therefore did not have their fee ready, had to wander the shore of the River Styx for a hundred years before Charon would let them on the

Having a seat in the Devil's Armchair.

boat.[74] You will not have to meet Charon in Mammoth Cave, but you may feel that he is lurking near the River Styx. You can hear the waterfall that bears his name, Charon's Cascade.

Lake Lethe–1842

In Hades, you would come to the River Lethe, the river of forgetfulness. Upon taking a drink from its waters you lose all memory of your previous life on Earth, and henceforth know only of the underworld.[75] There is no worry about losing your memory at Mammoth Cave's Lake Lethe; it is merely a pool of water left behind from when River Styx floods.

Devil's Looking Glass–1835

On the Violet City Lantern tour you are in a mysterious dim world of shadows where the only light is from a kerosene lantern. You cast your lantern light on a large, flat rock standing beside the trail. It looks unusual. Did it fall that way naturally? It looks too heavy to have been lifted into that position. In the flickering light, you see some old writing and marks with the date 1819 left by early visitors.

A closer look reveals something possibly more ancient beneath the nineteenth century graffiti. Drawn in charcoal are a stick figure and a zigzag line. Are they drawings of a person? A serpent? A lightning bolt? An ancient map? Is this the work of a prehistoric artist, or did an early nineteenth century visitor pick up a piece of an ancient torch to draw with? The drawings give the stone a mysterious and demonic look. An 1841 map refers to it simply as "D____'s Looking Glass" to avoid writing who it was named after.[76]

Infernal Regions–1844

Deep within Mammoth Cave's interior are the Infernal Regions, another name for Hell or the underworld. Infernal Regions made many cave visitors feel that Hell was where they had arrived. One 1844 cave visitor wrote, "If Devils dwelt on earth or within its bowels, we would suppose this a suitable place for their habitation and wherein to hold their orgies."[77]

Old Scratch Hall–1897

Part of the Infernal Regions is called Old Scratch Hall. Where better for Old Scratch (one of the Devil's many aliases) to reside? Nineteenth century guides apparently tried to convince tourists that the long scratch marks on the ceiling were the signature of Old Scratch himself. "The ceiling in Old Scratch Hall is marked all over in an extraordinary manner, which the guides assure us was done as a deed of darkness by the Evil One, although it looks as if they had done it themselves with the tips of their spiked staffs."[78]

Pluto's Dome–1893

Just beyond Old Scratch Hall is a great dome, a vertical shaft extending high into the ceiling. "Is this dome named for the Devil too?" the nineteenth century cave visitor may have asked. "No," the guide would reply. There would be a sigh of relief from a nervous traveler, anxious about being surrounded by so many devilishly named places. But then the guide went on, "It's named for Pluto, god of the underworld!" The name Pluto, ruler of the Greek world of the dead, was borrowed by the Romans and applied to their own underworld god. Eventually this dome and a planet were named after him.

Other names inspired by visions of you-know-who in Mammoth Cave include: Devil's Bathtub, Devil's Cooling Tub, Devil's Elbow, Devil's Turnpike, Devil's Pulpit, Devil's Punch Bowl, and Lucifer's Judgement Seat.

If all these Hellish names make you nervous about entering Mammoth Cave, remember this is one Hell from which people return. At least usually. Read on.

JUST PLAIN UNUSUAL

Some stories about Mammoth Cave do not fit neatly into any of the previous chapters, but they fit very nicely into the broad category of the unusual. Like the other cave stories, some of these are fact, some fiction, and some legend (a handy word to use when the tale may be a little of both.)

Nineteenth century cave guides enjoyed telling stories to raise a few hairs on the back of cave visitors' necks. Whether or not a story was actually true was not always regarded as important.

Guides talked about the stone-gobbler; a horse that lived in Mammoth Cave, ate stones, came to the surface at night, and made a noise between a gobble and a bray. The stone-gobbler could be useful. Once it ate all the stones in a farmer's field, enabling him to get a hundred bushels of corn where he got only ten before. People were warned not to shoot at the stone-gobbler; the horse could fling its head around and throw a stone at you farther than a rifle ball. An 1860s visitor from Philadelphia felt that even though some people believed the story, he was not convinced. "I found the legend of the

stone gobbler had obtained a good deal of credence . . .
to this was added superstitions of headless dogs, giant-
esses, oracular voices, grizzly bears and many sorts of
subterranean goblins."[79]

Robert Bird, who visited the cave in the 1830s, wrote
of a story he heard from several people in and around
Mammoth Cave. They told of an inn near Mammoth Cave
that had many travelers arrive, but few leave. Behind the
inn was a great cave with a terrible pit, the depth of
which was not known. The master of the inn took pleas-
ure in doing away with weary, unsuspecting travelers by
offering to take the guest's horse to the stable, then
leading the animal into the pit. He would run get the
horse's owner and tell him the horse had accidentally
stumbled into the cave and help was needed to retrieve
him. Upon getting the traveler to the pit the innkeeper
would push him to his death.

The writer expressed some doubt concerning the
truth of the story.

> I must confess that none of my infor-
> mants were very positive in their modes of
> telling the story, and none able to vouch for
> its truth; while a cautious, or judicious, per-
> sonage professed an entire disbelief in the
> innkeeper's guilt, hinting that the whole story
> had grown out of the wild prattling of a
> woman, the poor man's wife who was, in the
> narrator's opinion, a mere unhappy lunatic.[80]

This is not the only murder tale involving a pit. The
anonymous 1853 fictional story *The History of Ester
Livingstone and Dark Career of Henry Baldwin* is about
the vengeful adulterous Henry who visits Mammoth Cave
with his wife, Ester, who had murdered Henry's lover,
Naomi, a few days earlier.

"Come Ester," I said, "let us see if we can't make some discoveries in this quarter." Ester hung lovingly on my arm.

"Take care," said one of the guides, "if you go far you will be entangled among a number of passages that cross each other, and lose your way."

Sure enough, we did lose our way!

Our path terminated a yard before us on a jutting rock, which projected over a vast abyss. From the depth of this abyss ascended the moan and the sigh of a subterraneous river. . . . It was an awful sight. The torchlight flashed over the abyss, but could not light with one ray the river far, far below. . . . And our path ended in the rock which jutted over that fathomless abyss. . . .

"This is a cavern hitherto undiscovered," said I. "It is not described in any of the books; we are the first discoverers. Let us give it a name, Ester dear. What name shall we give it?"

"The cavern of the stars."

"A beautiful name," I answered, "but I know a better. Let us call it, the Cavern of Naomi!"

And I flung her from me, and urged her toward the edge of the rock, flaring the torchlight in her face.

"The Cavern of Naomi! For here the murderess of Naomi will meet her fate! . . ."

The horror, the livid despair of Ester's face, would have touched the heart of a devil, but it did not touch mine.

"Pardon! pardon!" and she fell on her knees, on the very edge of the cliff.

"Forgive! forgive! Oh, Henry!"

But I advanced upon her, and thrust the torch into her face. In withdrawing herself from it she stumbled and slid from the rock into the abyss, her death screams echoing horribly along the vast expanse. . . .

I held the torch over the abyss, and watched the flutter of the white garment which she wore, and heard her last cry.

And then I retraced my steps to the main avenue, (for I had not lost my way), and joining my friends, inquired after Ester, who, I informed them, had left me some hours before. They had not seen her. I was amazed, and then horrified. We searched for her for hours, but without success; and the next day, and the day after, and still our efforts were fruitless. Every one pitied me, the disconsolate husband—and I was to be pitied.[81]

Stories of rescues do not require murder attempts. Cave guide John Nelson wrote of an incident on the subterranean Echo River:

It was on January 17, 1904 that a party of seventeen, five women and twelve men followed me through the iron grated gate at the entrance of this massive underworld. We were starting on our trip to Echo River. Every man was bumping their heads on the cave roof. I knew that only a short distance further down the river the cave roof was higher and that shortly we would be where all parties could sit normally and I could resume the roll of the standing picturesque gondolier. . . .

One of my passengers suggested that we ought to raise the cave ceiling so the next party could come through. He accompanied the remark with a demonstration of just how the ceiling should be raised by putting his back against the ceiling as if he would push it up. Immediately the bow of the boat went beneath the water. Instantly the boat was filled with water. Every light was drowned out except the one I protected by holding up. Most of my seventeen passengers were floundering in the water of Echo River. The screams and the cries of terror were multiplied a hundred times by the echo of the cave. I pride myself that I did quick thinking. With the light in my hand, I tried to jump to a small nearby mud bank, but before I could do so, several pairs of arms were wrapped about my legs and shoulders. "Turn me loose," I shouted, "or we will all be drowned." But with the desperation of drowning men, multiplied by the darkness and strangeness of the surroundings, they clung on. I had begun to fight clear of the terror stricken passengers who were holding me when the resonant voice of Senator Muehlbronner was heard above the panicky screams, saying, "Attention; do as the guide says, or none of us will get out of here alive."

Some people say that drowning people will not listen to advice, but those wonderful people did. Again I cried out, "Turn me loose at once." And miracle of miracles, they did just that.

I made my leap to the mud bank and landed in the mud over my shoe tops, but, thank God, it was good Old Mother Earth I was standing on. . . . I grabbed the mooring chain of the boat, now submerged with most of my party in it or hanging to its sides, some still threshing in the water. With all my strength, and still trying to protect my one and only light, I tugged at the boat, and slowly with its frightened human cargo, brought the nose of the boat into the mud bank.[82]

The cave visitors were so glad to make it out of the river and cave alive they held a banquet for Nelson that evening in the Mammoth Cave Hotel and formed the Echo River Club to commemorate the event. Although members of the club were from the far apart cities of Cincinnati, Chicago, Pittsburgh, and Minneapolis, they gathered for meetings over the years in various cities including Philadelphia, New Orleans, and Boston. Whenever John Nelson attended the meetings he was given a hero's welcome. The Echo River Club was so impressed with Nelson's bravery that day on the river, the group had a medal made for him showing a boat and a fearless guide on Echo River.[83]

The long labyrinth like passages that lead cave visitors so far from the surface world inspired an 1830s author to write a story of another world deep within the earth's interior, that can be reached only through the deep, winding passages of Mammoth Cave. This land inside the earth received sun through openings in the earth at the North and South Poles. The human inhabitants used giant birds they called om-mos for transportation. The author gave the tale the lengthy title of, *A Wonderful Discovery! An Account of a Recent Exploration of the Celebrated Mammoth Cave of Edmonson County, Kentucky, By Dr. Rowan, Professor Simmons and Others, of Louisville, to its Termination Of the*

Earth.[84] The story is along the same vein as *Journey to the Center of the Earth,* but predates Jules Verne's famous book written in 1864 by twenty-five years!

In the Historic section of Mammoth Cave stands a giant coffin-shaped rock appropriately called Giant's Coffin. As your eyes take in this behemoth boulder, you spy a name carved on the lower left corner: J. N. McDowell M.D. 1839. You wonder if it could be so old. The signature is authentic. Many names written on Mammoth Cave's walls are that old and older. Even more interesting than the graffiti's ripe old age is the story behind the somewhat eccentric physician who carved it there.

Dr. Joseph Nash McDowell was a successful doctor, medical professor, and founder of McDowell Medical College in St. Louis, known today as Washington University.[85] He paid a visit to Mammoth Cave in 1839, the same year the cave was purchased by another physician, Dr. John Croghan.

Like Dr. Croghan, McDowell may have believed caves had healing properties. They were not the only ones who believed this. The idea that caves and their formations would cure various ailments has been held by many throughout history. It is said that Dr. McDowell became ill and believed himself to be at death's door. His medical partner, Dr. Charles W. Stevens and his son, Dr. Drake McDowell, vowed that when he died they would have his body placed in an alcohol filled lead casket suspended from the limestone ceiling of Mammoth Cave.[86] There is no need to ask a park ranger where you can see Dr. McDowell's casket hanging, because the vow (if even made) was not carried out.

The doctor's interest in caves caused him to purchase one near Hannibal, Missouri. According to legend, he suspended his deceased daughter's casket in the cave.[87] Perhaps he was familiar with the preserving properties of nitrates often found in caves and hoped they would

81

preserve the body. The story is that vandals broke into the cave, which caused McDowell to remove the girl's body, thus ending his experiment with cave burial.[88]

In McDowell's day, an adventuresome boy explored the dark passages of what was then called McDowell's Cave. His underground hijinks inspired him as an adult writer. Today the cave is not named after its nineteenth century owner, but after the writer—Mark Twain. The cave adventures mentioned in Mark Twain's books, *The Adventures of Tom Sawyer,*[89] *The Adventures of Huckleberry Finn,*[90] and *Life on the Mississippi*[91] (in which he mentions the casket incident) are based on his childhood experiences in McDowell's Cave.

Unusual things have been said to occur above ground as well as underground at Mammoth Cave National Park. In the early 1940s, several eyewitnesses claimed that a monster inhabited the Green River. The beast was said to be "as long as a joe boat" (about 12 feet), weigh as much as 300 pounds, and when it jumped, the water would splash 200 feet high. The water around Houchin's Ferry, which still carries cars back and forth across the river today, was supposed to be the monster's favorite hangout. A ferryman reported in 1941 that he had seen it many times, and gave a description.

> It's got a powerful big head. It could swallow a man without no trouble. Once it opened its mouth and I got a glimpse inside. I could have rolled a barrel—and I don't mean a keg, I mean a big barrel—in its mouth. It's got fins and tail just like any fish and eyes as big as horse apples setting in its head: it's got the longest whiskers or feelers you ever saw, and once when it jumped I thought I saw legs on its belly. But I can't rightly say about the legs.[92]

Do not rush to Houchin's Ferry in hopes of seeing the Loch Ness Monster's American cousin, for it has not been spotted in recent times.

Of course not everyone who visits Mammoth Cave meets crazed innkeepers, river monsters, mummies, devils, or ghosts. Nor do people tend to get lost and go insane. But knowing you are walking the passages where these stories originated can make your spine tingle. As the years go on other people will see things they cannot explain; strange new tales will arise. These new stories will be added to the list of oddities from America's most famous cave.

The Green River Monster.

NOTES

1. Wright, Charles W., 1860. *A Guide Manual to the Mammoth Cave.* Louisville: Bradley and Gilbert, pp.44-45.
2. Hovey, Horace C., 1880. 100 Miles in Mammoth Cave. *Scribner's Monthly Magazine*, Vol. 20. Reprint 1982, Golden: Outbooks, p. 23.
3. Lovecraft, H. P., 1965. *Dagon and Other Macabre Tales.* Sauk City: Arkhan House Publishers, Inc., pp. 322-328.
4. Mader, Joseph H., Circa 1946. *The Courier-Journal.* (Possibly never printed).
5. Olson, Rick, 1998. Personal communication. Mammoth Cave National Park, Mammoth Cave, Kentucky.
6. Bird, Robert Montgomery, 1838. *Peter Pilgrim or a Rambler's Recollections.* Philadelphia: Lea and Blanchard, pp. 134-135.
7. Shackelford, Oliver, 1920. Interview. Mammoth Cave: Mammoth Cave National Park Library.
8. Blake, Lillie Devereux, February, 1858. A Tragedy of the Mammoth Cave. *The Knickerbocker*, pp. 119-121.
9. Connor, Eugene and Samuel Thomas, 1966. John Croghan: An Enterprising Family Physician. *Filson Club Quarterly*, Vol. 40, pp. 205-234.
10. Gratz, Hyman, 1815. Green River, or Mammoth Cave of Henderson County, Kentucky. *Medical Repository of New York*, Vol. 17, N.S. Vol. 2, p. 391.
11. Bird, Robert Montgomery, 1838. *Peter Pilgrim or A Rambler's Recollections*, Philadelphia: Lea & Blanchard, p. 47.
12. Drake, Daniel, 1850. *Principal Diseases of the Interior Valley of North America.* Cincinnati: Smith, p. 240.
13. Forwood, W. Stump, M.D., 1880. *An Historical and Descriptive Narrative of the Mammoth Cave of Kentucky.* Philadelphia: Lippincott, p. 22.
14. Davidson, Robert, 1840. *An Excursion to the Barrens and the Mammoth Cave of Kentucky*, Lexington: Skillman, pp. 62-63.
15. Meloy, Harold, 1972. Medics at Mammoth Cave. Unpublished paper, Mammoth Cave National Park Library.
16. Hovey, Horace C., 1882. *Celebrated American Caverns.* Cincinnati: Clark. Reprint 1970, New York: Johnson Reprint Corporation, p. 81.

17. Jones, William, 1844. *Wonderful Curiosity: A Correct Narrative of Celebrated Mammoth Cave of Kentucky.* Russelville: Smith/Rea, p. 20.
18. Anderson, O. H. P., Letter from Small Collection #185. Kentucky Library, Western Kentucky University.
19. Wright, Charles, 1860. *Guide Manual to Mammoth Cave.* Louisville: Bradley and Gilbert, p. 23.
20. Knox, Thomas, 1874. *Underground, or Life Below the Surface.* Chicago: Burr/Hartford, pp. 466-467.
21. Tayler, Bayard, 1860. *At Home and Abroad.* New York: Putnam, p. 199.
22. Sides, Stanley and Harold Meloy, 1971. Pursuit of Health in the Mammoth Cave. *Bulletin of History of Medicine*, Vol. 45, p. 375.
23. Clifford, John D., September, 1811. Letter published in *Proceedings of the American Philosophical* Society, Philadelphia.
24. Mitchell, Samuel L., 1817. Commentary on Caves in Kentucky. *Medical Repository*, Vol. 18, pp. 188-189.
25. Gratz, Hyman, 1815. Green River, or Mammoth Cave of Henderson County Kentucky. *Medical Repository*, Vol. 17, pp. 391-393.
26. *Barnum's American Museum*, 1998. Internet site, Columbia University Department of Education.
27. George, Angelo, 1994. *Mummies, Catacombs, and Mammoth Cave.* Louisville: George Publishing Company, pp. 83-85.
28. Ward, Nahum, 1814-1818. Letters to Thomas Ward. American Antiquarian Society Collections, Worcester, Massachusetts.
29. Ward, Nahum, 1815. *Plan and Description of the Great and Wonderful Cave in Warren County Kentucky.* Buffalo: Salisbury Publishers, pp. 1-3.
30. Meloy, Harold, 1968. *Mummies of Mammoth Cave.* Shelbyville: Self published, p. 21.
31. Willis, Nathaniel Parker, 1853. *A Health Trip to the Tropics.* New York: Scribner, p. 156.
32. Wright, Charles W., 1860. *Guide Manual to Mammoth Cave.* Louisville: Bradley and Gilbert, p. 49.
33. Forwood, W. Stump, M.D., 1870. *Mammoth Cave of Kentucky.* Philadelphia: J.B. Lippincott and Company, p. 170.
34. Curator at Smithsonian Institution, 1998, 1999. Personal communication. Washington D.C.
35. Historical Collection Curator at American Antiquarian Society,

1998, 1999. Personal communication. Worcester, Massachusetts.

36. Morgan, C., 1911. Reminiscences of Mammoth Cave. *Hart Count Herald.* pp.1, 4.
37. Postcard, New Entrance Hotel Proprietors, circa 1922. Louisville, Kentucky.
38. Robbins, Louise, 1970. A Woodland Mummy from Salts Cave, Kentucky. *American Antiquity*, Vol. 36, pp. 200-206.
39. Pond, Alonzo, 1936. *Lost John of Mummy Ledge.* Madison: University of Wisconsin, Department of Anthropology, Professional Publications Series.
40. Morgan, C., 1911. Reminiscences of Mammoth Cave. *Hart County Herald.* pp. 1, 4.
41. Bullitt, Alexander Clark, 1845. *Rambles in the Mammoth Cave.* Louisville: Morton & Griswold. Reprint 1985, St. Louis: Cave Books, pp. 12-13.
42. Thompson, John, 1909. *Mammoth Cave Kentucky.* Louisville: Courier-Journal Job Print. Reprint 1985, St. Louis, Cave Books, pp. 15-19.
43. Smith, Nathan Ryno, 1869. *Legends of the South.* Baltimore: Steam Press of William K. Boyle, pp. 45-46.
44. Turner, James, 1872. A Visit to Mammoth Cave. *Canton Weekly Register*, Canton, Illinois.
45. Pursell, Larry, 2000. Personal communication. Beaverton, Oregon.
46. Lyons, Joy Medley, 1996. Personal communication. Mammoth Cave National Park, Mammoth Cave, Kentucky.
47. Wood, Kerry, 1996. Personal communication. Mammoth Cave National Park, Mammoth Cave, Kentucky.
48. Spradlin, Neila, 1996. Personal communication. Mammoth Cave National Park, Mammoth Cave, Kentucky.
49. Gray, Jamie, 1996. Personal communication. Mammoth Cave National Park, Mammoth Cave, Kentucky.
50. Hanion, Charles, 1996. Personal communication. Mammoth Cave National Park, Mammoth Cave, Kentucky.
51. Cutliff, Lewis, 1996. Personal communication. Park City, Kentucky.
52. Nardacci, Michael, 2000. Personal communication. Albany, New York.
53. Flowers, Sarah, 1996. Personal communication. Mammoth Cave National Park, Mammoth Cave, Kentucky.
54. Lyons, Joy Medley, 1996. Personal communication. Mammoth

Cave National Park, Mammoth Cave, Kentucky.
55. Brucker, Roger W. and Richard A. Watson, 1976. *The Longest Cave.* New York: Alfred A. Knopf, pp. 244. Reprint, 1987. Carbondale: Southern Illinois Press.
56. *Reinterment of Floyd Collins.* 1989. National Park Service News Release, Mammoth Cave National Park, Mammoth Cave, Kentucky.
57. Cassidy, Billy, 1997. Personal communication. Park City, Kentucky.
58. Murray, Robert K. and Roger Brucker, 1979. *Trapped! The Story of Floyd Collins.* Lexington: The University Press of Kentucky.
59. Lawrence, Joe, Jr. and Roger Brucker, 1975. *The Caves Beyond.* New York: Funk & Wagnals. Reprint, Teaneck: Zephyrus Press, pp. 151-152, 155.
60. Cetera, Robert and Zona, 1997. Personal communication. Mammoth Cave National Park, Mammoth Cave, Kentucky.
61. Leek, Candice, 1999. Personal communication. Mammoth Cave National Park, Mammoth Cave, Kentucky.
62. Hanion, Charles, 1997. Personal communication. Mammoth Cave National Park, Mammoth Cave, Kentucky.
63. White, William, 1998. Personal communication. Petersburg, Pennsylvania.
64. Wood, George, 1997. Personal communication. Ft. Worth, Texas.
65. Palmer, Arthur, 1996. Ghosts Underground?. *CRF Newsletter*, Vol. 24, pp. 5-6.
66. Hagan, Susan and Michael Sutton, 1996. *The Mammoth Cave Gazetteer.* St. Louis: Cave Research Foundation.
67. Shackelford, Oliver, 1920. Interview. Mammoth Cave: Mammoth Cave National Park Library.
68. Meriam, Ebenezer, February 21, 1844. Mammoth Cave. *New York Municipal Gazette*, p. 319.
69. Bird, Robert Montgomery, 1838. *Peter Pilgrim or a Rambler's Recollections.* Louisville: Lea and Blanchard, pp. 117-119.
70. Alighieri, Dante, 1980. *The Divine Comedy of Dante Alighieri.* Danbury: Grolier Enterprises Corp., p. 13.
71. *The New Oxford Annotated Bible,* 1946. New York: Oxford University Press, p. 1501.
72. Bullitt, Alexander Clark, 1845. *Rambles in the Mammoth Cave.* Louisville: Morton & Griswold. Reprint 1985, St. Louis: Cave Books, p. 81.

73. Trip, Edward, 1970. *Crowell's Handbook of Classical Mythology.* New York: Thomas Y. Crowell Company, p. 159.
74. Zimmerman, J.E., 1964. *Dictionary of Classical Mythology.* New York: Harper and Row, pp. 58-59.
75. Trip, Edward, 1970. *Crowell's Handbook of Classical Mythology.* New York: Thomas Y. Crowell Company, p. 344.
76. Hagan, Susan and Michael Sutton, 1996. *The Mammoth Cave Gazetteer.* Cave Research Foundation.
77. Ibid.
78. Ibid.
79. Anonymous, 1867. From Philadelphia to Mammoth Cave. *The Philadelphia Inquirer.*
80. Bird, Robert Montgomery, 1838. *Peter Pilgrim or a Rambler's Recollections.* Philadelphia: Lea & Blanchard, pp. 101-103.
81. Anonymous, 1853. The *History of Ester Livingstone and the Dark Career of Henry Baldwin.* Philadelphia: Elmer Barclay, pp. 35-36.
82. Nelson, John, Date unknown. Former Cave Guide Has Story of Echo River Boat Accident. Clipping from Glasgow, Kentucky Newspaper, Mammoth Cave National Park Library.
83. Mader, Joseph H., Circa 1945. Unpublished special to *The Courier-Journal*, Louisville, Kentucky, Nelson family Collection.
84. Anonymous, 1839. *A Wonderful Discovery! An Account of a Recent Exploration of the Celebrated Mammoth Cave, in Edmonson County, Kentucky.* New York: R.H. Elton, pp. 12-18.
85. Valentine, Mary T., 1894. *The Biography of Ephraim McDowell, M.D.* Philadelphia: Self published, p. 158.
86. Brodman, Estell, December, 1980. The Great Eccentric. *Washington University Magazine*, December, 1980, p. 11.
87. Twain, Mark, 1883. *Life on the Mississippi.* Boston: James R. Osgood. Reprint 1992, New York: Book-of-the-Month Club, pp. 451-452.
88. Thomas, Samuel, Eugene Conner, and Harold Meloy, 1970. A History of Mammoth Cave Emphasizing Tourist Development and Medical Experimentation Under Dr. John Croghan. *Register of the Kentucky Historical Society*, Vol. 68, pp. 328-329.
89. Twain, Mark, 1876. *The Adventures of Tom Sawyer.* Hartford: American Publishing Co. Reprint 1976, *The Unabridged Mark Twain.* Philadelphia: Running Press, p. 554.

90. Twain, Mark, 1885. *The Adventures of Huckleberry Finn.* New York: Charles L. Webster. Reprint 1976, *The Unabridged Mark Twain.* Philadelphia: Running Press, p.752.
91. Twain, Mark, 1883. *Life of the Mississippi.* Boston: James R. Osgood. Reprint 1992, New York: Book-of-the-Month Club, pp. 451-452.
92. Meloan, Jack, 1941. Sea Monsters?. *The Courier-Journal,* December 7, 1941, Louisville, Kentucky, pp. 9-10.